How To Make 30k A Year Cleaning Windows

Pete Harris

pete-harris.com

© Pete Harris 2015

Table of Contents

About The Author

Hello and firstly I would like to thank you for purchasing my book and welcome you on your first step to setting up and running a successful Window Cleaning Business.

My name is Pete Harris and I have been a Self-Employed Window Cleaner since January 1991. When I started the country was in a recession as it is now (at this time of publication 2012) and I decided to close down the Market Trading Business that I was operating because quite frankly no body was spending any money on the markets and I could not compete with the big high street retailers.

There was very little chance of securing a job anywhere and as I had been self- employed for a couple of years I had really got use to the freedom of working for my- self so I tried to think of another business that I could setup that did not require a lot of money (mainly because I did not have a lot) and could yield me a good living.

Also I had very little technical skills as I had previously been employed in an administration environment but still managed to come up with an idea. Yes you have guessed by now, I started to clean windows and quite frankly I have never looked back and regretted a single minute.

I set up my business for less than £ 100.00 and was earning more money in 2 days than I was getting working 7 days a week on the market.

Throughout this book I will draw on my personal experiences but will endeavour to give an impartial and unbiased perspective on all the pros and cons of firstly being self-employed and secondly just what it takes to maintain a Window Cleaning Business.

By the end of this publication I will deliver a blueprint on how you could potentially earn in excess of £ 30,000.00 per year with very little initial outlay and overheads.

"Where There's Muck There's Money"

Introduction

I would like to welcome your to your first step on a journey that will end at you having in your hands a blueprint to a £ 30k Business. That is a bold statement but is 100% achievable.

One of the best aspects to this business is that you can set this up for under £ 150 and use the vehicle that you already have.

There is no need for previous experience and any costly training program to go through as well as very low day to day running costs. I will show you how for under £ 10 a day outlay how you can earn £ 130 + a day.

Does the thought of starting at 9am and being at home by 3.30pm including having the freedom of a lunch break appeal to you?

I thought So!

Did you know that there are in excess of 26 million households in the UK, so there is a great big pie out there for you to get a slice of? Also I can assure you that even in this time of recession the simple fact is that people are still prepared to pay someone to clean their windows. I set up my business way back in 1991 when the situation regarding the state of the country's economy was very much similar to what it is now. In actual fact in 1995 I relocated and I set up the business again and don't worry it does not take very long.

Anyone, male or female, young to let's say more mature people can do this. I will show you how.

I have thought long and hard on how to actually write this book. Therefore I have constructed it in a way that each chapter will be formatted in the form of a question that you should be asking yourselves, in respect with that I have decided to write you an answer to that question hence providing you with the solution that you can take away and implement.

I will draw on my own experiences over the last 20 years or so, sharing the mistakes that I have made and how I overcame them.

So without further ado let's get started and I will finish on one of my favourite sayings and believe me there is so much truth in it.

WHERE THERE'S MUCK THERE'S MONEY.

What Are Your Goals

It is very important that you are clear in your mind exactly what your goal is.

Ask yourself firstly how much money you need to earn. Is this going to be a full time business or are you going to run it in conjunction with another business or employed job that you may be currently undertaking.

Are you going to operating as a sole trader and working on your own or are you looking to build a larger business in which you will be employing people and your role will be more of a managerial role and overseeing the running of the company.

Is it your objective to build up multiple rounds so in time you can sell them on? I will be sharing with you links to websites that you can buy and sell Window Cleaning Businesses. I have seen businesses listed that turnover less that £ 1000 a month being offered for sale for many thousands of pounds that is something that you may not have thought as possible.

Is it the lifestyle of being your own boss, not being told what to do and when to do it? That for me is why I like this business. You are out in the fresh air, seeing different people every day, working the hours that I want and the clincher is that every day is a payday.

It is important to have a clear timeframe in mind that you need to have the business up and running. Believe me that it does not take a long time to build a business and get a regular cash flow coming in.

Take some time to create a list of the goals that you want to achieve. When you have completed create multiple copies that you can have within easy reach. For example keep one in your car or van, so that when you are at work and maybe you are having a bad day, which you will, you can read through it and reenergise yourself why you are doing it.

Also keep on in your office or study area, or a shortcut icon on your computer. It is a really useful tool to have within arm's reach so that you are able to refocus on what you are aiming to achieve.

Be clear on what start-up capital you have at your disposal and keep to it. I will show you how you can get up and running for under £ 150, I will also show you equipment that can cost in the region of £ 500+ which will be what is called Pure Water Fed Systems. Also as I stated earlier I will show you resources that you can buy a business to really fast track your success.

I can show you all this but there is something that is totally out of my control. That my friend is YOU. It will be up to you to take on board what you will learn, to implement these steps and to have the motivation to go and get the work and then do it. What you will be building is a long term business. A business that once established will be a very valuable asset. This is not a get rich quick scheme. It's a very honest business that yes does require hard work but the rewards are extremely favourable.

In the next chapter we will be looking into how you are going to get your customers and build up that valuable customer data base.

What Is Your Marketing Strategy

Paying customers are obviously the life blood of your business. Get this part, and what we will be talking about in the next chapter about pricing, right is the most important part of setting up your business. You will only ever have to do this once. At some point you will find this tedious and you may get dejected but you have to push through this.

Let me give you one example to whet your appetite.

The first customer that you get signed up is for a £ 12 job. At first you may think that £ 12 is not a lot of money but if you times that by 12 which is how many cleans you will do in a year the value of that customer is £ 144. When you consider this the process of canvassing is well worth it.

Let's take it on one step further. If on your first day canvassing you get 10 people to sign up at £ 12 a time that is £ 1440 of work a year. I would like to think that that would give you motivation to go out and do that again the next day and so on. It's is a rinse and repeat strategy.

Right let's look at the various methods used in order to sign up paying customers.

Canvassing

This is my favourite way and you will find that it is the most effective way of building up business. My advice would be to pick an area or housing estate that is local to where you live. The reason I say this because firstly you don't want to be travelling to far because at the end of the day time is money and the quicker you can get to work the better, secondly in these days of high petrol prices you don't want the expense to be eating into your profits.

It is important to look professional both in appearance and organisation. They say that first impressions go a long way to how people perceive you. So look smart and talk with authority. Be organised. Make up a folder with an A4 pad to list what streets you are planning to target and record what houses answered the door and the outcome of that meeting and which ones there was no answer from so that you can follow up again at a later date.

Also it is advisable to have some fliers printed so you can put through the door of the houses that there was no answer from so that when you door call back the householder can put a face to who delivered the flyer. Also another good tip is to have some business cards printed, because you will find that people are not able or prepared to make a decision there and then and will ask for your contact details. By giving them your card it will reassure them that you are genuine and professional.

It is vital that when you have anything printed to include your mobile number, your landline number and your full postal address. People will be more prepared to trust you if they have these details at hand. Also it is important to have it clearly stated that you are fully insured just to give that little bit more of professionalism. We will talk about insurance in a later chapter.

If you look online you can find many printers where you can get a couple of thousand fliers and a few hundred cards printed for around about £ 30. This is well worth the investment.

When you have your first contact with a potential customer it can be quite daunting. You may stumble over your words but this is natural so do not worry. My approach would be on the lines of this.

"Hello there, my name is (your name) and I am starting up a Window Cleaning Business and I was wondering if you would like to have your windows cleaned on a regular basis"

Now the most common answer will be "Sorry I already have a window cleaner"

Do not get discouraged and don't leave it there, I would then say "Ok thanks very much, could I leave you one of my cards just in case you ever get let down you can feel free to contact me".

The reason I say this is that a lot of people will say they have a window cleaner when in fact they have not; it's any easy excuse to say. What you will find that some people will look out for you when you start cleaning in their area just to see if you are reliable and will then approach you. So bear that in mind.

The next answer you will get is "I clean my own thank you". Again ask if you can leave them your card in case they ever decide to stop doing them themselves.

Then you will get the golden nugget answer "Yes I would be interested, can you give me a quote?"

This is it, you are in and this is where what we will be talking about in the next chapter about pricing up the job.

As I have said you will feel nervous when you first start to canvass but in no time it will seem like common nature and it will be rolling of your tongue and the more confident you be become.

Canvassing can be time consuming but is far the best way to start as it is low cost and you get the feel of dealing with people and when you get that first customer signed there's no better feeling because with one customer you have a business. Then the snowball effect will happen, your business will get bigger and bigger as more people sign up.

One last thing to bear in mind is that there will be other window cleaners operating in the area that you are canvassing. Don't let this put you off, competition is good, it means that there is a need for your services as any one person can only do a certain amount of work, there is plenty out there for all of us. One golden rule which will go into more in the next chapter is never undercut someone else, you are just opening yourself up to hassle that you just don't need.

Advertising

Advertising is very effective and come fast track you onto building up your business. The thing is this method costs. When looking at this method you will be approaching your local newspapers. I know that in my area, which by the way is Norfolk, my local paper charges around about £ 14 a week. That is £ 728 a year. That is serious money so if you go down this route, if you get people ringing you up make sure you ask where they got your number from so you can analyse if it is worth it. If you are getting 5 new customers a week which are averaging £ 12 a time, obviously it is worth it. Also what you need to think about is that once you have got a full round set up, then there is no need to advertise any more. I myself have never advertised in the local papers so I really am not in a position to tell you to do this or not. All I can say is that I have set up two window cleaning rounds so I will leave you to make your own mind about this.

If you do advertise then there are some common rules as having printed material produced. You must have this information within your advert –

Name

What Service It Is That You Are Offering

Contact Numbers

Address

State that you are fully insured

Have a guarantee – "Satisfaction Guaranteed"

A logo is optional but sometimes keeping it nice and clean and simple works better than anything else.

Fliers

Fliers can be effective but you have to bear in mind that people sometimes get so much advertising material through the letter box that a lot of people don't even look at it and it goes straight in the bin. Saying that, again if you look online for the printing of fliers, you can get around 5000 printed for under £ 50. You could get your local newspaper to put say 2500 within their next publication and distribute them for their readers and see what response you get. If you get one person signed up for £ 12 then that is £ 144 over a year, it's a bit of a no brainer.

The thing is you are going to get more than one customer ring you up out of 2500 leaflets being distributed. I can remember when I did it I was working on around about 3 – 4% response rate, that means 3 – 4 people out of every hundred were contacting me. Now out of that 3 – 4 % not everyone is going to take you on after you been to see them and given them a quote but I feel confident in saying, as I have experience of this, that half of them will. So that means that you end up with a 1.5 – 2 % success rate.

Let's do some maths

1.5% of 2500 is 37.5 so we will round it up to 38

38 x £ 12 = £ 456 x 12 cleans a year = £ 5472 a year

2% of 2500 is 50

50 x £ 12 = £ 600 x 12 cleans a year = £ 7200 a year

As you can see the figures add up very favourably.

The disadvantage of this method is that unless you are very lucky the location of the people who contact you may be a bit varied and not grouped together. The flip side is that it will get you into areas that you may not have thought of and you can tap into the potential of that area by canvassing it. Also it can save you some serious leg work because you will know where there is a demand for your service. It's well worth it if you have the capital at your disposal.

Signwriting of your vehicle

This is advertising on the move. Yes it does cost money initially but once it is done look at it as free advertising. I have a medium size panel van and had a quote for the two sides and the back doors to be sign written. It would have cost me £ 140, which I thought was ok but I did not have it done as quite frankly I don't need any more work as I am very well established. What I did do though a few years ago was I made up some very basic signs and put them in the side windows of an estate car that I had. Basically I got some bright yellow paper, made the signs up with all my contact details, laminated them and put them inside the windows. See there is always a cheap option to get your point across.

The good thing about this method is that you always have got a physical presence. Whether you are at work, parked in the local supermarket, on the high street or at home potential customers can see you all the time.

Word of mouth

Nothing else compares to this but as I am sure you can understand this takes time. If you are good at your job and you are reliable then your customers will recommend you to family, friends and people who they meet.

What can be better than this? You are getting all the benefits without having to do any leg work and you do not have to pay anything out. It's like gold dust.

There is one more method that I would like to share with you but I must warn you it is very rare.

Luck and being in the right place at the right time!

This is what happened to me. I used my local supermarket for fuel and got friendly with the cleaning supervisor as he was always cleaning them pumps when I pulled in to fill up the car. He was telling me that the company that he was working for were having trouble with the window cleaning part of the contract that they were servicing. Basically, and I mean no disrespect, they had the general cleaners doing the windows and they did not know what they were doing. He asked me if I would be interested in talking to his Area Manager about sub-contracting the window cleaning. I said that I would. We arranged a meeting and to cut a long story short we agreed a price and I took over the window cleaning aspect of the contract.

I started off with 10 supermarkets and when they found out, and I am not being big headed, how good I was because they were not getting marked down any more they gave me another 11 to make a total of 21. I was getting up at 3.30am

Monday – Friday so that the stores were cleaned by 8.00am when they opened. I must admit that I could not cope with that number so we settled on that I would cover 16. I serviced this contract for just over 2 years until the company that I was sub-contracting off lost the contract due to the chain of supermarkets (Somerfield) being sold off.

See I was in the right place at the right time and took advantage of the situation and opportunity that was placed in front of me. It was very hard work but the rewards were very welcoming but it did come with one or two problems which I will go into in a chapter when I talk about residential and commercial work.

Well I think I have covered in great detail the various method of obtaining work. Some methods cost you absolutely nothing which is what I am trying to get over to you. You can build up a business without laying out any money, but if you want to get on a bit quicker and have a small amount of money you have a few opportunities to fast track yourself to success.

In the next chapter we will look at the important aspect of pricing up the work.

What Is Your Costing Structure

So Just How Are You Going To Price Up A Job

Although this is one of the fundamental aspects of your business it is relatively straight forward and simple. What I am also saying is that it's not an exact science. It is something that like canvassing, once you have done it a few times it becomes second nature. When you become more experienced you will know straight away how long a job is going to take you. I am not going to spend too long on this because quite frankly there is no need to.

What I will say now is you need to be looking at turning over at least £ 25 an hour. Now I can imagine you are thinking that I am mad saying that. I can assure you that I am not, this is relatively easy to achieve and in a moment I am going to show you how. Before I do I would just like you to consider this. At the moment of this publication (September 2012) the current national minimum wage rate is £ 6.08. The average hours that people work is 37.5.

Based on these figures the minimum wage for a full weeks work is £ 228.00. Now I would never belittle this figure because I know that there are thousands of people who work extremely hard for this amount of money and I have full respect for them. What I would say is in my opinion is that this is nowhere near enough money for people to live on, however that is out of my control. What I can show you is how you can potentially earn more than that in 2 days working a maximum of 6 hours a day!

I still to this day, after over 20 years doing this for a living, struggle to think of another job or career that you can do that you can earn you this level of money, that requires no qualifications and no training, saying that you can go on training courses but believe me you do not need to, the reason I say that is I never have had a minutes training. There is a knack to doing this job which, you can self-teach yourself with practice. When I first started I had the cleanest windows on my street as I kept going over them again and again until I had got the knack, it only took me a couple of days and I was confident to go out and charge people for my services.

Right I am going to stop waffling now and tell you how much to charge, I just wanted to assure you that I have been sitting where you are now so I can relate to all the thoughts and concerns that you are experiencing.

I am sure that you have noticed in previous chapters that I keep referring to charging £ 12 for a clean. Why I say this is that you should be looking at an average customer value of £ 12. Let me make it clear if you were to go and quote £ 12 for a one bedroom flat you would never get any work, also if you were to quote £ 12 for a five bedroom county side barn you would probably have to work in excess of 60 hours a week to make a living and I am pretty sure that you don't want to do that.

I have based this figure on an average 3 bedroom semi-detached family home because that is what I live in. It has 8 windows, 2 patio doors, a front door and back door. That adds up to 12 individual windows to clean. So my recommendation is to charge £ 1.00 a window. See I told you that is was simple. It's a relatively easy house to do as there are no awkward windows to get at; it has a flat roof over the porch, so there is easy access to one of the bedrooms.

This is a very easy property to clean and it will only take you 20 minutes to do once you get into the swing of it. My advice is for you to try and get properties like these because you can really rattle through them and get the money rolling in.

I know that is easier said than done as properties come in all shapes and sizes. In my own business I have properties ranging from a one bedroom sheltered housing bungalow to a 6 bedroom mansion situated on the Norfolk Broads, as well as car showrooms and high street shops. So as I have already said you will get to know how long each particular job will take so price accordingly but always have in the back of your mind the hourly rate of £ 25 that you want to be hitting.

Here are some other prices for you to bear in mind that you will encounter when pricing up.

Standard 2 pane window - £ 1.00

Bay windows - £ 2.00

2 pane Leaded Windows - £ 2.00

Patio Doors - £ 1.00 for each door

Hard to reach windows (ones that particular care which will take longer) - £ 1.50

When I say hard to reach never ever put your-self in danger. I personally do not get onto sloping roofs because when I first start started back in 1991 I was a little bit naïve and did not realise the risk and fell off a porch roof. Now that was only about 8-9 feet but that's high enough. Luckily I did not break anything but I severely bruised the tendons in the arch of my foot. Subsequently I could not put any weight on it for a week so that means loss of earnings.

You will find that a lot of new houses built today have sloping porch roofs with windows above them. What I tend to do is put the ladder up the side of the porch and if I can't reach the window with having one foot on my ladder and reaching across, I inform the house owner that I can't do that particular window and adjust the price accordingly.

You will find that the vast majority of people will accept that no problem, you will always get some people that huff and puff but stand your ground and if it is required walk away from the job, it simply is not worth it.

This scenario is totally taken away if you decide to go down the route of what is called Pure Water Fed Pole Systems. We will talk a lot more about this in a forthcoming chapter, but basically you can reach up to 60 feet with telescopic poles, taking away the need to use ladders as you can operate from ground level.

What I would like to talk about now is you should never under value your- self.

 What do I mean by this? You will find that when you give someone a price most of the time people will give you a simple "yes" or "no". If you get someone say "no" it is very easy, and I am talking from experience, to start to start taking a pound of here and there, especially when you first start out. I am telling you now don't. Some people will expect you to do that, they like to think they have got one over on you if you relent. If they don't want to pay you what you want then walk away, there will be someone just around the corner more than prepared to pay your price, please trust me on that one.

You will also from time get the ones who, if you have quoted £ 10, will say "my last window cleaner only used to charge £ 5" (don't you just love them). I can remember once I had quoted

£ 8 for a house just off Great Yarmouth seafront, the owner said to me "I only used to pay £ 2 before", I said "I would not get out of bed for £ 2" and walked away. I now that does not sound very professional and perhaps I should not have said that but it gave me a lot of satisfaction.

The point I am making is that I remained in control of the situation and was not going to be dictated to by some idiot, because that's what those sorts of people are. What you have got to remember is that you are in business, you are not doing this as a favour to the home owner, you are doing it for you and your family.

What I want to talk about now is what you exactly do for the price you are charging. Some people might think that when you clean a window it means you only clean the glass. WRONG! If you want to be classed as professional then what you do is wipe down the frame, clean the glass including the corners and wipe the window sill down. Whatever you do don't leave cobwebs all over the place and soap suds on the sill. This is the reason you can justify charging £ 1.00 for a standard window.

Make sure that you point this out to the home owner. Incorporate this into you sales pitch; tell them that you are not like most window cleaners who only do half the job. Most windows nowadays are UPVC so it's very easy to keep the frames clean; it only takes a few seconds to wipe them with a damp piece of Scrim. My philosophy is if you are going to do a job then do it right or don't bother. If you can work with that attitude then you won't go far wrong.

The only other thing I can think about pricing is what we call "The first clean".

When you take on a new customer it is very likely that the windows will be in a bit of state. They may well have not been cleaned for years. It is perfectly reasonable for you to charge more for the first clean. As long as you explain it clearly then the home owner will be perfectly reasonable about this. It is worth taking that bit more time on the first clean because it makes what I call regular maintenance cleans so much easier.

So for arguments sake if the normal cost of the clean is going to be £ 12, then for the first clean charge them £ 18, that is 50% more, remember you are in business. Make a good job so that the customer is happy and are satisfied that they have got their money's worth and I can assure you the next clean will be a piece of cake and you will fly round.

For commercial jobs it really is up to your discretion on how much to charge. There really is not a text book commercial job. The range of jobs is vast. It may be the local corner shop or up to what I do and have done. For example car showrooms or supermarkets. There are many factors to take into consideration, frequency as some businesses may want them cleaned on a weekly basis, so if you were looking at a job what you would usually charge £ 25 then it may be in your interest to charge them only £ 20 if they want it done weekly because that is £ 80 a month in your pocket for one customer as regards to having to find 4 customers.

Also you may want to look at the nature of the business. An accountant, solicitor or estate agent would think that are more prestigious than say the local newsagent so charge them more because they are more likely to pay it. There is nothing wrong with that.

The Golden Rule

I have touched on this earlier. Never undercut another window cleaner. I have never done it, hand on heart, and I never would.

I have had it done to me. Some people think the grass is greener on the other side. I have lost jobs for the sake of 50p, how sad is that? The thing is when they get let down or they don't get the job done as well as what you do they want to come back. Well I will let you make your own decisions on that but I have never taken anyone back. Its gives me so much satisfaction to say "No" because quite frankly I don't need people like that, as far as I am concerned they have done it one they will do it again.

Also if you do undercut someone else you are opening yourself to all kind of hassle. You better be able to look after yourself as I have heard stories of people who have really taken exception and have made sure that the under cutter has not been able to climb a ladder. I shall say no more.

There is nothing wrong with going onto areas where window cleaners operate. I have many a time been cleaning a property and talking to a window cleaner who was doing the one next door. There's plenty of work for everyone and you soon get to know your fellow colleagues. You will get some who don't want to talk to you but you get that in every walk of life.

I must admit I did not think I would be talking about pricing as much as I have but there is something that I want to bring to your attention. There are 2 different business models which you can base your business on.

The 4 Week Model.

This is where you clean properties on a 4 weekly basis.

The average customer value would be £ 12.

The Pros

Fewer customers needed so faster to set up.

Easier to organise and manage as the work schedule will be the same month after month.

More of a routine.

The Cons

None.

The 8 Week Model.

This is where you clean properties on an 8 weekly basis.

The Pros

You are perfectly justified in charging more for each clean. It can be a selling point that although the individual clean will be more as it will take longer, where in reality it won't, the cost per month will be less as it is spread over 2 months.

Therefore I would suggest that you charge 25% more.

This then bring the customer value up to £ 15.

Ultimately your business is worth 25% more for not working any harder.

The Cons

You need double the amount of customers so it will take longer to set up.

You will need more management and organisation because the work schedule will alternate month to month.

I know many window cleaners, some work on the 4 week model and some work on the 8 week model. I know one who incorporates both models. I personally work on the 4 week model because I like the fact that I do not need as many customers. That is what I have always worked to and I can't see me ever changing. Within my business I offer other services that I offer so I do not need the extra customers. I will talk about that later on in the book which may be of interest to you.

Fundamentally both models work very well so it is really a matter of personal choice and whatever you are happier doing.

What Are Pros and Cons of Window Cleaning

I will start off with the positives that relate to having your own window cleaning business and also self-employment in general.

The Pro's

You are the boss

Basically you are your own boss so there is no one telling you what to do, where to do it and when to do it. You control every aspect of your business and you live and die by the decisions that you make. Don't let that frighten you, instead accept the challenge and meet it head on so you get in the mind set of being a businessman. Once you have that professional attitude making decisions will become easy.

You get to choose the jobs that you want to do. Whether it is residential or commercial you have the flexibility to take on the work you desire. There have been times when I have been asked to price up work and when I have assessed it has not really taken my fancy and that can be for many different reasons.

What I do is one of two things, either say that I am not interested full stop and walk away or if I feel that there may be something in it for me, but it has to be on my terms, is to price it up in my head what I would normally charge and then double or even triple it. If the person says no then fair enough, I am not really that bothered, if on the other hand they accept the price it then becomes a good earner. I have found that this works for me. At this point in my business I can afford the luxury of picking and choosing jobs, however when you are starting out it may be a case of taking what you can get.

Choosing the hours that you want to work.

This is great because you have the flexibility of starting and finishing when you want. No more 9 – 5 schedules. My typical day is starting at 9.30 in the morning and being home by around 3.30 in the afternoon. Some people may think that I should and could work longer and they are entitled to their opinion. However because I choose the profitable jobs and price them correctly then I don't need to work any longer than these hours. I am a great one for sayings and slogans and one of my favourite ones is "Work Smart Not Hard".

Now I am not saying that I never work out of these hours because sometimes I do. It pains me to work on a Saturday because I think weekends are for enjoying yourself, but if I get the opportunity to earn very good money then I will. In my opinion working on a weekend is overtime so I price accordingly. I would at least double my rates for these jobs because if the client wants the job done then they will pay what I ask. This may sound a bit clinical but you are running a business not doing someone a favour.

A Regular Income

Having a window cleaning business is fantastic because once you have your round up and running you know exactly what income you have coming in month after month. It is not like other trades such as plumbing, decorating or building where you are reliant on the next job and waiting for the phone to ring. You will have a core number of clients that you visit regularly, whether that is on a 4 weekly or 8 weekly basis. Plus you will earn money every day, no more waiting until the end of the month for your wages or waiting for the cheque for the job that you have completed which can sometimes take up to weeks or months to arrive. Your business will always have cash flow which is so important for any business to survive.

A Business that is personal

What I mean by this is that you form a relationship with your clients. You will have some people that you get on better than others and also you will have favourite ones as well. You tend to get involved with different aspects of their lives, as they do with yours. With what makes them tick, who you can have a laugh with and you will becomes friends with them.

Many times I have gone out for a drink or had a game of golf with my customers which makes this business so nice. They look forward to seeing you as you do them. Because I have been doing this for so long I can remember when customers have had children which have now grown up into adults and who have now had children themselves. I can't think of many other businesses that have this personal element to them.

You get all the rewards

There is a saying "You only get on in life through hard work". That is very true but I have been employed in many jobs where I have worked very hard for someone and got very little appreciation in return and yes they have paid me a wage but now where near what I have earned for them.

Well that all stops the moment you become self-employed. You only get out what you put in but the reward are 100% yours. If you are prepared to work hard you can go from minimum wage to £ 25 per hour and it is all yours.

Job security

You may not have even considered this but being a window cleaner gives you so much more job security than being employed. Think about it, in this time of economical tension with so many businesses closing down there are hundreds of thousands of people, and you may be one of them, who are constantly thinking about whether they will still have a job this time next week, next month or next year.

You will never have that worry again. Yes there will be times when people drop out of your round through various different reasons, they may have lost their job, they can't afford it any more, they may move and sadly the client has passed away.

But consider this if you lose a customer you have not lost your job, that customer will easily and quickly be replaced. To lose your job would mean that something catastrophic would have to happen. Your whole client base would have to drop out at the same time and you can trust me on this that will never happen. Your business will be your job for life or however long you want to carry on doing it.

The Cons

The Weather

This is by far the biggest obstacle that you will encounter when you become a window cleaner. Don't get me wrong it is lovely when the sun is shining but the British climate as we all know can be somewhat temperamental. Working outdoors in the winter is very challenging. Saying that it can be done.

Rain

You can work in the rain but you have to know when to draw the line. Drizzle and steady rain when it is just falling down straight is fine and workable. If you find the rain is pelting down, horizontal and crashing into the windows then quite simply don't even bother. You can't do the job properly and your customers will not be happy if you turn up and you are likely to lose them.

Snow and Ice

You can work in snow and ice but without stating the obvious you have to be careful. If you have a good portion of bungalows and ground level work then you should have no problem working. Obviously the condition of the roads is a contributory factor to whether you can travel safely.

Extreme Cold

What I mean by this is the air temperature. In extreme cold conditions you will find it may be impossible to work because when the water, even if it is warm at origin, comes into contact with the cold glass it will freeze. One tip would be to add some anti- freeze to the water, that is your choice but in my experience when the conditions are that cold you really don't want to be outside working.

Sunshine and warm conditions

Now you may be a bit surprised that I have added this but there is a reason. Working in the sun is really nice but it does come with some challenges. When you put water onto glass in direct sunlight and warm conditions it dries really fast. If you are not quick this can affect the quality of the job. It can lead to smears as effectively the squeegee blade is passes over dry glass. The trick is to make sure you put enough water on and if cleaning large areas of glass is to do it stages. This all comes with experience. Also as a result of having to work quicker you ultimately become hotter within your body but the trade-off is that you get the opportunity to get home earlier to enjoy that cold beer in your garden.

What you have to realise that when working out- doors you will encounter all these conditions and you will learn to adapt. What you also have to accept is that there will be times when you will be sitting at home unable to work, that I am afraid goes with the territory.

Collecting your money

This can sometimes be a little bit annoying but in all my 20+ years I have never let it become an issue. Before you take on the life of being a window cleaner you have to accept that your customers will not be in every time that you call. What I do is leave a note to say that I have cleaned the windows today and will call back at the end of the week. Because all of my work is located in the same town I will always be passing by to stop and collect what is owed.

What you will find is that when people get to know you they will leave the money out in pre-arranged places. I never specifically go out to collect money in an evening as you are using fuel that you would not usually use; therefore it is cutting into your profits. If after a week or so I have not managed to catch a customer in I simply will leave it until the next time I call to do the windows.

Because I have been doing this so long and have long standing routines and agreements with my customers I never have more than 5% of my weekly turnover owing at any given time, so as I have said it has never been an issue.

Some people send me cheques; some people actually call round to my house to pay me. I can honestly say that in all my years of doing this for a living there has been no more than 20 times when people have not paid me. The policy that I operate is never to let a customer get in arrears of 3 cleans which is in time wise 2 months. You soon get know if you are going to have any trouble getting money out of people and all I can advise is as soon as the alarm starts to sound in your head then drop the customer.

I have had more hassle with businesses and commercial work than I have ever had with residential customers when it comes to payment. I will talk more about that in a later chapter.

Unhappy customers

You are only human so you will make mistakes, that is only natural and you should not see that as failure. This usually occurs in your early days of being a window cleaner. I am not being big headed but I don't get any complaints, but that is only because I have been doing this for over 20 years so by now I should know what I am doing, that is fact.

If you do get a complaint always ask them to show you what you have done wrong, there is nothing wrong with that. If it turns out that you have not done the job correctly then fair enough, simply apologise and do the next clean for nothing and the customer will be happy.

There is a saying "The customer is always right ", sorry I don't agree with that. There are some dishonest people out there who go out of their way to get something for nothing. If you know 100% that you have done nothing wrong, don't give a refund, simply say that you don't agree with them and you will be removing them from your list and walk away. That is what I have done in the past and it has never affected my business or reputation.

No sick pay or holiday pay

This relates to being self-employed in general. You will wake up some mornings and feel under the weather but you don't have the luxury of calling the office and taking a sickie and if you are very lucky still getting paid for it. If you don't go to work then you won't get paid. As far I am concerned I have to be half dead before I don't go to work and if you want to work for yourself then I suggest that you get into that mind-set.

As regard to holiday pay, then yes you have guessed it, you don't get any full stop. Saying that you can book your holiday whenever you want which is some compensation. If you run your business correctly you will be able to afford to take time off. I have nearly 6 weeks holiday a year!

Injury

I feel that I have to make you aware that when using a ladder there is a risk that at some point you may fall off. There is no easier way of saying it but don't let that put you off. I have once but that was in the first few weeks of starting, so that was well over 20 years ago. Basically I had the ladder at a too shallow angle so that the bottom slid away as I walked up it. I only fell about 8 feet but that is high enough, I didn't break anything but severely bruised my foot which in turn stopped me working for about a week.

You have to always be aware of your safety and the general public around you. It is advisable to take out some insurance for yourself and the public which we will cover in a later chapter.

In the next chapter I will be talking about the equipment that you will need.

The Equipment That You Need

In this chapter I will be talking about what equipment that you will need to run you window cleaning business.

Vehicle

Basically any vehicle is suitable to run your window cleaning business. I am assuming that you already have a vehicle which obviously cuts down the initial costs of setting the business up.

You can use anything from a small hatchback to a medium size panel van. I started with a hatchback and the only thing you need to get is some roof bars so that you can carry your ladders. I have had estate cars but now run the business out of a medium size panel van.

Ladder

I have a three stage extension ladder. It is compact but still enables me to get up to heights of around 20 feet, which is more than adequate for residential work. Any way you don't really want to be working any higher than that off a ladder.

Traditional Window Cleaning

Squeegee

The squeegee comprises of three components.

The Handle

The Channel

The Rubber Blade

I use a standard 12 inch channel and blade for residential work and a 20 inch system for commercial work. The blades are interchangeable and reversible and I buy them in 38 inch strips and cut them down as it is more cost effective.

Applicator

The applicator comprises of two components. The T Bar and Sleeve.

A Bucket

I think that is self-explanatory.

A Scraper

This is used for scraping bird deposits of the glass. It is advisable to use this rather than to rub it with the applicator to eliminate scratching the glass.

Scrim

This is a linen based cloth which is used to detail the edges once the soapy solution has been removed from the glass. Also it is recommended to have a separate piece which is used solely to wipe the frames down.

Towels

These are used to wipe the actual window sill as a final procedure.

Washing up Liquid

It is essential that you use a high quality concentrated washing up liquid. Don't use a cheap one because quite simply you will not get a professional finish.

Water

This is an obvious statement. What I suggest is that you carry your own water. Why I say this is when I first started I had arranged to do this house as my first ever job. The trouble was when I turned up to do the job the person was not at home, so therefore I could not clean the windows. From that day I have always carried my own. Another reason is that a lot of homes have water meters and you could find that people become funny about supplying you with water and might ask for discounts.

And that is it. It is hardly rocket science and complicated. Nothing mechanical or electrical so nothing can break or let you down. The only thing you have to do is change the rubber blades when they wear out.

Pure Water Fed Systems.

Pure water fed systems is a different kettle of fish all together. There are many companies which will provide complete systems which will purify the water which is the used to clean windows through telescopic pole systems which have brushes attached. The process means that water is sprayed onto windows then agitated with the brushes and then rinsed down. The windows are then left wet and after a period of time they dry to a crystal clear finish. This process virtually eliminates the use of ladders as windows can be cleaned from ground level.

Systems come in various guises which include backpack, trolley and completely installed van systems.

The main components of these systems are as follows.

Reverse Osmosis Unit

These units are designed to remove dissolved solids and micro-organisms from any water supply. They typically remove between 90 – 90% of dissolved solids to produce high quality water to perform the procedure of cleaning windows without any the need of any chemical detergents.

Filters

These remove chlorine and other compounds from the water supply.

Water Pump

Water pumps ranging from 60 – 100 psi to pump the water to the brush head.

Hoses

Hoses are used to run up the water fed poles.

Water Fed Poles

These are telescopic pole systems that can range from 4 feet to 27 feet which virtually eliminate the use of ladders.

Brushes

These come in various shapes and sizes which can also be changed to different angle to reach awkward windows.

Water tanks

Come in various capacities for either trolley systems or van mounted systems.

Batteries

Used to power the pumps to give water pressure.

Trolleys

Used to carry the water tanks on portable systems.

Water Quality Meters

Used to check that the quality of the water is sufficient to perform the task.

As you can see there are lots of components needed to work these systems. As these are mechanical there is always a risk of the systems failing and breaking down which obviously can affect your earnings. As I have said there are many companies that sell these systems and it is vital to that before purchasing that you get some relevant training so that you are completely confident with the operation of the equipment.

In the next chapter we will be talking in more detail about the two cleaning methods. Traditional or Pure Water.

Which method should I use? Tradition or Pure Water

This is a very important decision which you need to make. Here I will explain what both methods entail and the pros and cons for each method.

Traditional window cleaning is something that most people will be familiar with. It is very low tech and a very low cost option in order to set up your window cleaning business.

The process is very simple with the application of a soapy solution onto the window which is then removed with a rubber blade which we refer to as a squeegee.

This method does not require any particular training as I regard it as a knack, not a skill. It is something that comes with practice and eventually experience. When I first started out I basically practiced for hours on my own house until I got it right. The best tip that I can give is to make sure you put enough water onto the glass and always keep the squeegee moving. This will drastically reduce the chance streaks and smears appearing, but as I have said just practice, practice and practice some more.

It is vital to use professional standard equipment and high quality cleaning solution. Do not be tempted to use the cheap £ 2.99 squeegees from your local diy store because they do not give the finish that is required. The reason I say that is because that is exactly what I did and it does not work. Cutting corners only leads to problems arising and will cost you more money in the end.

Pure Water Window Cleaning

This can be quite technical because of the process needed to produce the pure water and the equipment that is needed to perform the task of the cleaning the windows. It can also be very expensive with systems ranging from many hundreds of pounds to thousands of pounds.

Basically you purify water that comes from your house supply which is then stored in tanks, either in your garage or directly into a van.

The water is then applied to the windows through water fed pole systems either directly from your vehicle or back pack and portable trolley systems.

You first rinse the frames and glass, and then you agitate the glass with brushes before finally rinsing the glass again and the window sills. Then the windows are left to dry naturally to a crystal clear finish.

Which is better?

That is a question that basically has no definitive answer. They both work as well as each other. I will try to explain, in my opinion, where they both have advantages and disadvantages.

Firstly I will make one thing clear. I only use the traditional method within my business. I have physically used the pure water system that a friend of mine uses and I can confirm that is does work. But it is a matter of choice that I have not implemented into my business because after doing it the traditional way for over twenty years I do not have the inclination to change and have to explain the process to my existing customers.

What I will say that that when I take on new customers, a good portion ask me if I do it traditionally or the pure water way. The reason they ask is that they only want it done the traditional way because they don't like the pure water method. The reason for that is they dislike the fact that the windows are left wet and don't feel that it gives as a professional finish. Basically they like the frames and windows to be completely dry, that is what they expect. This is the main reason I have not changed because my customers are happy with the way I do the job so why rock the boat and potentially upset anybody.

As you are in the position of starting out you have the opportunity to choose. The pure water system is regarded to be a quicker method than traditional. Each method is as only good as the operative, meaning they only work if you do it right. It also relates to the type of work that you take on to which method is better.

Let's say you have a two bedroom bungalow to clean which takes you 10 minutes to clean using the traditional method, is it really worth the hassle of running say 100 feet of hose from your van or unloading a trolley system, getting everything into position and that's before you start cleaning anything, only to then when you have finished have to pack everything away again. I think not, in my opinion you could have the job, moved onto the next and finished that one as well.

On the other hand if you have a building with hard to reach windows then it is obvious that the pure water system would be the best option.

My business consists of mostly residential clients and as I have said before I am quick at my job and personally I cannot see the benefit of the pure water system in my business. It all depends on what work you want to target.

I can really see the benefit of the pure water system within the commercial work sector. When I was doing the contract work cleaning supermarkets I would have definitely used it, alas it was not around then. It would have certainly made my life a lot easier.

My personal opinion is that if you are doing what I say standard family homes then I would go traditional. If on the other hand you are specialising in standalone country barns or houses that are large in size then it may pay you to opt for the pure water system.

If you are going to solely do commercial work such as supermarkets, libraries and office blocks then pure water is the only method to choose.

Another thing to take into consideration is the amount of water that you use within both methods and the effect to the environment. The companies that sell the pure water systems may imply that it is better for the environment because no chemicals such as detergents are being used in the process of the cleaning the windows compared to traditional. That is true but the amount of water that is needed to perform a day's work is significantly more using pure water compared to traditional so that is hardly environmentally friendly, is it?

In conclusion it is matter of various factors to consider to which system you use. Your own personal preference and that of your customers, the cost of setting up your business and the type of work that you will be undertaking. Both methods work and have their own place in the market place.

In the next chapter I will be discussing the pros and cons of both residential and commercial work.

Essential Information

This chapter is dedicated to, although boring, essential information which you need to be aware of when starting out in business. This information is generic and not just applicable to window cleaning.

This information is related to the United Kingdom. If you are reading this another country then you will have to check with your tax laws and regulations.

Registering your business

First of when you start working for yourself I suggest you apply to become a sole trader. There is no need to be a limited company and you will not need to register for VAT unless your turnover is over the threshold. At the time of this publication (February 2015) the threshold for VAT is £ 77,000.

What you need to do is contact H.M.R.C or visit their website where you will find out all the information need about starting up your own business.

Accounts

Self-employed people come under the Self-Assessment taxation system. This means you pay tax twice a year, at the end of January and at the end of July.

You are responsible to provide accounts for the H.M.R.C and your tax return has to be submitted by the end of January every year. It is highly advisable that you employ the services of an accountant. This is not very expensive as the accounts for a window cleaning business are quite straight forward and you have the peace of mind that they are finalised by a qualified person. The accountant will also fill in your tax return and submit it online so it is on the tax office system instantly.

Basically your accounts will show your total earnings and your expenses for the year. The expenses are deducted from your turnover which then leaves an amount which is your profit which is the amount that you will be taxed on.

It is vital to keep all receipts and records of all outgoings which you have relating to the day to day running of your business. Your accountant will be able to advise of everything that you can claim for and there will be a lot of things that you would never have thought of.

Bank Account

It is your own personal choice if you have a Business Account. I have never had a business account for my window cleaning business.

Business accounts incur charges and they eat into your profits.

Insurance

I would suggest that you look into taking out two types of insurance.

Public Liability Insurance

In this current environment of insurance claim culture it is advisable to have some form of Public Liability Insurance. I won't go into everything it covers, quite simply it is easier for you to read the fine print within the policy, but it covers you for injury that a member of the public could attain because of an action that you have caused within the undertaking of your job. It could also cover you for damage to property that you may be working on.

If you take on contract work then on many occasions this will be compulsory and you will have to provide proof to the organisation who is issuing the contract.

Personal Accident and Injury Insurance

This is for you. You are now self-employed with no safety net of a company sick pay scheme so it is up to you to cover yourself. There are many schemes on the market which you can obtain direct from the insurance companies. Alternatively you could contact an insurance broker to explain what scheme is best suited to yourself or even they can be available at your local bank.

They are well worth having as you are potentially putting yourself at risk of injury or sickness.

Your £ 30k Blueprint

Start Up Costs – The costs listed are an average of products available and it is wise to shop around to get the best value.

Traditional Window Cleaning

18" Applicator Sleeve £ 10.00

18" Applicator T Bar £   6.00

Squeegee Handle   £   8.00

12" Channel   £   5.00

Squeegee Rubber   £   2.00

Scrim   £   6.00

Washing Up Liquid   £   2.00

15 Litre Bucket   £   7.00

3 Section Ladder   £ 104.00

Total   £ 150.00

Water Fed Pole System

25 Litre Trolley System   £ 820.00.

The 4 Week Business Model

Your aim is to get an average customer spend of £ 12.00.

Therefore the weekly amount of cleans that you need to do is 55.

So the total number customers that you need are 220.

This will give you a turnover of £ 660.00 per week.

You work 47 weeks per year which allows you to have 5 weeks holiday per year.

This gives you an annual turnover of £ 31,020.00

The 8 week business model

Your aim is to get an average customer spend of £ 15.00

The number of weekly cleans is the same – 55.

The number of customers required will double – 440.

This will give you a weekly turnover of £ 825.00.

Again you work 47 weeks which allows you to take 5 weeks holiday per year.

This gives you an annual turnover of £ 38,775.00.

The choice is yours, both models work as well as each other. The first option is designed to get you up and running quicker but the revenue yield is less, whereas the second the second option will take considerably longer to set up but the rewards are much more.

There is a little bit of housekeeping that I need to do now and that is in the form of an earnings disclaimer. Please read the following carefully.

Disclaimer

FINANCIAL AND INCOME RESULTS ARE BASED ON A WIDE RANGE OF VARIABLE FACTORS. I HAVE NO RESPONSIBILITY OR WAY OF KNOWING HOW WELL YOU WILL PERFORM, AS I DO NOT KNOW YOU, YOUR BACKGROUND, YOUR ETHIC OF WORK, OR YOUR ABILITIES, PRACTICES OR SKILLS. THEREFORE, I DO NOT GUARANTEE OR IMPLY THAT YOU WILL BE FINANCIALLY WEALTHY OR RICH, THAT YOU WILL DO AS WELL AS I DO OR EVEN MAKE MONEY AT ALL. THERE IS NO GAURENTEE YOU'LL DO AS WELL IF YOU RELY UPON MY INFORMATION AND FIGURES. YOU MUST ACCEPT ALL THE RISK OF NOT PERFORMING AS WELL.

Moving forward

When you have reached the level of having a full quota of customers that does not mean that that is the end of you earning potential.

You have to think like a businessman/woman. You have a list of clients who month after month pay you money for your services. What other services could you provide to extract even more money out of them?

Let me give you some ideas. Well they are more than ideas as I actually implement them into my business.

Carpet Cleaning

Every one of your customers has carpets in their home. Carpets are a very expensive investment and they need to be maintained to prolong their life cycle.

There are many companies who provide training and equipment packages which you can purchase for under £ 2000.00. Now that may sound a lot of money but I can assure you that there is a lot of money in carpet cleaning and you can easily recoup that investment very quickly.

Pressure Washing

Patios, driveways, paths and decking all become very dirty especially after winter so this income stream could become a nice addition to your business.

You can purchase very high quality machines for under £ 500.00. Again like carpet cleaning you can earn very good money very quickly.

Gutter and Fascia Cleaning.

I love this so much. The reason being is that you can literally do this on a shoestring. You can add this to your business for under £ 50.00. All you need is a hose and a telescopic brush. Yes you can invest in vacuuming and observational equipment which can cost hundreds of pound, but you don't need to, I never have. You will be amazed at what you can earn doing this.

There you have three additions to your business, you will have the clients so you can market these services and it won't cost you a penny, and I am sure that you will have find that there is a huge demand.

These additions can also be standalone businesses.

I have every intention to publish books on how to start up these businesses in the near future so please keep an eye out for that.

Please check out the resources page where there will be information on websites for equipment and training that is available.

Also there is one more method to increase your turnover that does not require any more customers or hard physical work.

Increasing your prices

The trick to this is not to do it every year because your customers will become savvy. I increase my prices every 2 years without fail. When I first increased prices, many years ago, I was frightened to do it because I thought people would stop having me, you may have the same concerns. Trust me there is no need to worry.

As long as you do every couple of years your customers won't hold it against you. I often have people asking me when I am putting up the price.

It's time again for some quick maths.

I will work this out on the 4 week business model.

Right I have said that you need 220 customers at £ 12 a time.

What I would advise you do is increase the price by £1.

That is an increase of £ 220.00 every 4 weeks.

You will on average clean people's windows 12 times a year.

12 x 220 = £ 2640.00 wage rise after 2 years.

I am sure that you will agree that is a good increase.

What I will say is that you will get the odd one who doesn't like it. As far as I am concerned they have got two choices and it doesn't bother me which one they make. If they drop out then there is always someone to take their place.

There is one last thing I would like to bring to your attention, and that is selling your business. Your business is a valuable asset which many people are willing to pay you a lot of money for. The longer that your business is established for the more money that you can ask for it.

This is something that I have never looked into with any great detail but it is something that will be of interest in the future.

Conclusion

In my opinion window cleaning is a wonderful, stress free and lucrative business to set up and operate. As I said at the beginning of this book, I started in this industry as a stop gap while the business that I was operating was going through a downturn in trade. What I found out was that window cleaning was a much more viable way to make a living, and a decent one at that. I am 100% sure that I made the right decision for me and my family and definitely have no regrets.

Every one of you who has read my book will have different reasons for purchasing it. You may have recently lost your job or you may be unhappy with your current working environment and are looking for a way out. You may have always wanted to be your own boss and are looking for a low cost option that does not incur a lot of risk. You may have another business and are looking for a way to earn a second stream of income. The list of reasons can go on and on.

What I will say is that you will find it hard to find a business that is this easy to set up. This is a real physical business that once you have got your customers, you can see in black and white, month after month what you will be earning and as I have shown you, you can add different services to offer a complete cleaning package.

It is hard work physically. You will have days when it is cold when you would like to be indoors in the warm. The thing is to stick at it, success doesn't happen overnight. You are building a business that you will become proud of. When you get to that position you will feel an overwhelming sense of satisfaction.

So I would encourage you to take the bull by the horns and go for it. You never know it may be the best decision that you have ever made.

Finally I would just like to again thank you for purchasing my book. I hope that you have enjoyed reading it and that has given you lots of positive things to think about. If you take action then I wish you all the very best for the future.

Good luck

Pete Harris

pete-harris.com